Spirits of the North

Two-legged, Four-legged, Winged, Finned, Rooted, and Flowing

Northern Exposures from Alaska, Yukon, B.C., and the NWT

by Kathleen M.K. Menke

**All Photos/Contents
©Kathleen M.K. Menke/Crystal Images**

Published and Distributed by Crystal Images
PO Box 781, Haines, Alaska 99827
www.akmk.com   ci@akmk.com   907-766-3517

ISBN 978-0-9764261-2-7
First Edition 2010

Published in the United States of America
Printed in China through InterPress Limited

Cover Photo: *Friends Laura Firth and Tabatha Nerysoo walk home from church on a bright late summer Sunday in Fort McPherson, Northwest Territories (NWT), Canada.*

Bald eagle, Chilkat Bald Eagle Preserve, Haines, Alaska

Raven on the tundra, along the Dempster Highway, Yukon

Eagle and Raven are the twin spirits, yin and yang, opposite moieties of Tlingit and other Native cultures of the Pacific Northwest. These spirits complement and complete each other. They can be found venturing their individual ways, communing among their own kind, interacting with their opposites, or mingling among a diversity of other spirits. It is a gift to be in their presence.

This book is dedicated to those whose souls have been touched by the spirits of the north.

Arctic ground squirrel demonstrates its tree climbing skills, Denali National Park.

Ground squirrels may sometimes climb surrounding shrubs and trees to access the fresh greens of spring. Here an Arctic ground squirrel perches among the branches of a leafing willow growing along a roadside overlook near the East Toklat River in Denali National Park in early June. Willow leaves are rich in vitamins and minerals. The willow leaves are a particularly good source of Vitamin C and are also rich in Vitamin A, calcium, and zinc.

Introduction

Those who live in the north, visit the north, or merely long for and love the north, have already formed their own connection with the spirits that reside here. This book is composed of images that portray spirits that have impressed me on my own personal journey through the regions of Alaska, the Yukon, British Columbia (B.C.), and the Northwest Territories (NWT). Though each person's journey in the north country is unique, encounters in this region consistently bring forth emotions that resonate deeply within one's soul.

Images selected for this book exhibit elements of the north that speak to me of personality and spirit--the two-legged, four-legged, winged, finned, rooted, and flowing. They are part of who I have become in my own northern adventures. They are, for me, a connection to place and to spirit.

Alaskans and Canadians, the two-legged spirits of the north, are tied closely by geography, cultural traditions, and lifestyles. While transitioning from one part of the north to another and through history and time, one finds that the people here are bonded to the land and to each other, strong within their individual creative spirits while being an integral part of the whole.

Animal spirits of the north enrich the landscape with their inherent wisdom and strength of character. They frequently have strong pair and family bonds. They exhibit curiosity, creativity, planning, strategy, and play. They know how to adapt and how to survive. One can encounter a ground squirrel doing nothing, it seems, but admiring the view of a morning sunrise reflected off Denali, be deeply impressed by the way a mother moose will go full force against a bear chasing after her young, or surprised by the responsiveness of a porcupine or beaver to a human voice.

Birds on the wing soar high on warm thermals and fly directly into gale force winds with apparent ease. They speak to each other with a multitude of vocals. Once they have brought their young to fledgling stage, the parents continue to nurture, providing ongoing lessons of survival. Male and female spirits share duties and adopt specific roles in the raising of offspring. Migrators know when to head north, when to head south, and where to find the best smorgasboard of late-run chum in November. Some have mastered the art of flying in formation. Juveniles of the season find both the way and the stamina to travel thousands of miles to the right destination for the first time.

After spending years in the open ocean, salmon return to the exact river in which they were spawned. Plants bend to the sun, draw in spring moisture, and know just when to drop their leaves as winter approaches. They carry the characteristics of being rooted, reaching deep into the soil, flexing with the wind, and growing as high into the atmosphere as far as climate and weather conditions allow them.

Spirit, the creative force infusing everything, permeates beyond the plant and animal world. Mountains lift, dominate a landscape, erode, change moods. Glaciers rumble, tumble, and recede. Rivers, lakes, and ponds freeze and break-up, babble, creak, murmur, and roar. The wind howls. The northern lights dance. The tides ebb and flow as the oceans cradle their own individual spirits. Each rock has an ancient story to tell. The spirits represented within this book are not easily defined or categorized, reminding us that all spirit flows, transforms, and interrelates. Each single moment represents its own eternity.

KmKm

Spirits of the Northwest Territories

Robert Alito welcomes visitors to Nitainlai Territorial Park Campground and Visitor Center just north of the Peel River in the NWT.

Nitainlai Territorial Park is one of many Yukon and NWT rest stops along the 400 mile long Dempster Highway that heads north from the Klondike near Dawson City in the Yukon to Inuvik just shy of the Arctic Ocean in the Northwest Territories.

Alito invites campers into the center in the mornings for coffee and stories drawn from the history of his local Teetl'it Gwich'in culture.

Traditional subsistence fishing boats line the shores of the Peel River, NWT. The free territorial ferry in the background provides summer transport for Dempster travelers.

Whitefish and cony (inconnu) hang drying in Noel's smokehouse at Tsiigehtchic along the banks of the Arctic Red River. The village of Tsiighetchic, where the Arctic Red River meets the Mackenzie River, has a long history as a summer fish camp for the Gwichya Gwich'in (people of the delta).

Percy Kay from Fort McPherson, NWT, picks berries on the tundra north of the Arctic Circle just south of Richardson Mountains and the Yukon/NWT border.

Spirits of the Tombstones

Tombstone Territorial Park along the Dempster Highway in the Yukon presents many faces to those who pass this way.

Established by the Tr'ondek Hwech'in, First Nations people of this area, and managed through an agreement between the Tr'ondek Wech'in and Yukon Territorial government, the Park encompasses 1,300 square miles (2200 square kilometers) in the south Ogilvie Mountains. This plan protects the natural and cultural values of the area while recognizing the Tr'ondek Hwech'in's traditional and ongoing use in developing and managing the Park.

The Park includes a concentration of diverse ecological niches providing habitat for an abundance of wildlife, uncommon at this latititude. Fox, moose, caribou, Dall sheep, black bear, grizzly bear, and dozens of species of birds inhabit this place. Berries are abundant in late summer and fall.

A public campground provides basic services. The Interpretive Center, open from late May to mid-September, offers displays, walks, talks, and general information on the Park.

Tombstone Mountain is the dominant landform of the Park, but the area also contains a great diversity of rocks, minerals, and geologic formations including a variety of seldom-seen permafrost landforms such as pingos, palsas and patterned ground.

View toward the Tombstone Mountains across the North Klondike River Valley of Tombstone Territorial Park, Yukon, early morning, September

Spirits Along the Dempster

Double rainbow breaks the storm, highlighting Goldensides Mountain, Tombstone Park, Yukon.

Oasis in the taiga, a few miles south of Eagle Plains, Yukon

Cross-fox, Tombstone Park, Dempster Highway, Yukon

Moose at dusk, Two Moose Lake, Dempster Highway, Yukon

Ptarmigan in the tussocks, Blackstone Uplands, Yukon

Spirits above the Arctic Circle

Autumn tundra and Richardson Mountains at the Arctic Circle along the Dempster Highway, Yukon

Arctic lingonberries and reindeer lichen

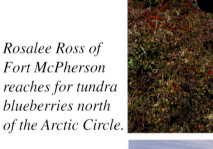

Rosalee Ross of Fort McPherson reaches for tundra blueberries north of the Arctic Circle.

Arctic crowberries and red bearberry leaves

Emma Kay, of Fort McPherson enjoys outing with her family in a berry patch of the Arctic.

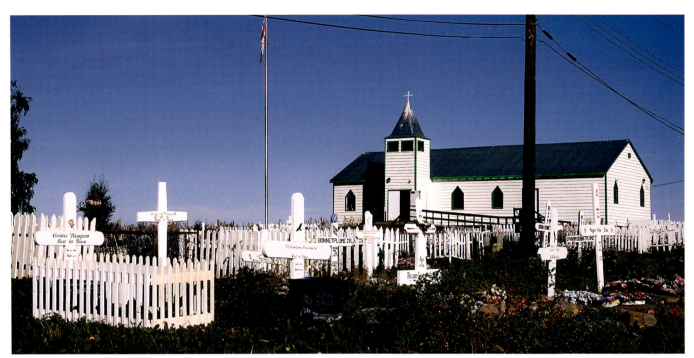

Saint Matthew's Anglican Church and Cemetery shine under a clear blue sky in Fort McPherson, NWT.

Located along the Peel River between the Mackenzie River Delta to the north and the Richardson Mountains to the south, Fort McPherson is the traditional home of the Teetl'it Gwich'in (people of the headwaters), a nomadic people who moved to follow seasonal hunting, fishing, and foraging opportunities. The traditional name for the community is Teetl'it zheh, named after the Tettl'it njik, the Gwich'in name for the Peel River. The graveyard next to the Anglican Church is the final resting place of the "Lost Patrol" of the Royal Canadian Northwest Mounted Police who perished in the harsh winter of 1910-11 while on sled dog patrol.

Friends Laura Firth and Tabatha Nerysoo walk home from the church above on a bright late summer Sunday. When asked for permission to take their photo, they responded with quick wit and a laugh, "Yes. Hurry, before we get too old."

Spirits of Inuvik

Midnight sun hangs in the north, Inuvik, late August.

Sebina and Michael, German motorcyclists, at Inuvik

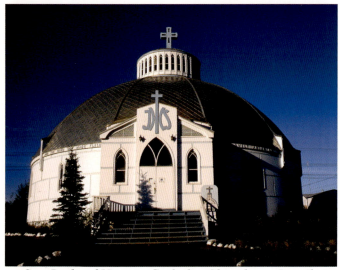
Our Lady of Victory Catholic Church, an Inuvik landmark, is often referred to as the Igloo Church.

Tatiana waters plants at the Inuvik Community Garden, housed creatively in a former hockey arena.

Mackenzie River Delta view north and west from lookout tower at Jak Territorial Park, south of Inuvik

Midnight Spirits

Northern lights dance above Nitainlai Territorial Park, NWT, late August.

Peel River sunset glows fiery at midnight near Nitainlai Territorial Park, NWT, late August.

Rooted Spirits of the Yukon

Young poplar shows its autumn colors along the South Canol Road, September.

Aspens along the trail from Klondike Highway overlook to Five Finger Rapids, Yukon

Spirits of the Klondike

Magpie near Riser Lake, Klondike Highway

Hiker, following the path of the gold seekers of 1898, pauses in the area known as "the scales" near the summit of Chilkoot Pass.

Canada geese and scaups gather in pond near Dawson City, Yukon.

White Pass and Yukon Railroad train approaches tunnel on route from Skagway to White Pass.

Tour guides pause for refreshment along the banks of the Yukon River, Dawson City, Yukon.

Spirits of Reflection

Early morning scene in the Blackstone Uplands along the Dempster Highway, Yukon

Lone scaup swims in the sunset, Yarger Lake, Tetlin Wildlife Refuge, Alaska.

Beaver on the edge of pond in the uplands area of Denali National Park, Alaska

Denali and the Alaska Range at Reflection Pond, Denali National Park, Alaska

Adventurous Spirits

Four Yukon members of a Kluane-to-Chilkat bike race team cap their Saturday summer solstice 150-mile bike race relay with a Sunday hike up Mount Riley on the Haines Peninsula. Hikers are facing north towards Mount Ripinski and the Takshanuk Range with the Chilkat River to their left, the community of Haines, center, and the Lynn Canal and Lutak Inlet to the right.

Kirk Sweetsir, popular Arctic bush pilot refuels his Cessna 185 at Arctic Village, Alaska.

Backpackers Jill Golden and Drew McCalley, flown into this remote area by Sweetsir, enjoy a rainbow across the Aichilik River Valley of the Arctic Coastal Plain of Alaska.

Spirits of the Arctic Coastal Plain

Birthing grounds for barren ground caribou, nesting area for thousands of birds, and home to a diverse variety of Arctic plants and animals, the 1002 area of the Arctic coastal plain of Alaska, just east of Prudhoe Bay, remains protected at the time of this writing as part of the Arctic National Wildlife Refuge (ANWR).

Here a grizzly bear prowls restlessly in search of food, perhaps a ground squirrel, along the banks of the Aichilik River. *Aufeis,* overflow ice, remains in the river bed throughout the summer here and elsewhere along Arctic rivers that flow north from the Brooks Range to the Arctic Ocean. Permafrost lies just inches below the surface of the summer groundcover of wildflowers, sedges, and cottongrass tussocks.

The Arctic tundra, like the alpine tundra, supports a great diversity of small plants that come into brief and vivid bloom in late June and early July. Multitudes of insects and birds are attracted here at this time. The caribou with their newborn calves begin their southern migrations.

For days surrounding summer solstice, the sun circles around, low in the sky for twenty-four hours. Arctic poppies bend their faces to follow the sun. Butterflies and moths fold their wings on landing to maximize warmth. Cocoons on the ground stir to life. For a few brief weeks, plants flourish and animals with their young eat well. The strong, with their diversity of adaptations and mirgration patterns, survive the winter.

Grizzly prowls across the Arctic Coastal Plain along the rim of the Aichilik River, late June.

Spirits in Bloom

Dwarf willow catkins, Denali N.P.

Alpine forget-me-nots, near Toklat, Denali N.P.

Shooting stars, Chilkat River estuary, Alaska

Capitate lousewort, alpine tundra, Denali N.P.

Skunk cabbage, Valdez, Alaska

Salmonberry flower, Southeast Alaska

Wind flowers, anemones, displaying purple undersides following a rainstorm, Denali N.P.

Bluebells, Reflection Pond, Denali N.P.

Pasque flower, Miles Canyon, Yukon

Calypso orchid, Southeast Alaska

Lapland rosebay (Rhododendron), Denali N.P.

Pasque flowers, Miles Canyon, Yukon

Labrador tea, near Wonder Lake, Denali N.P.

Field of Arctic poppies, Highway Pass, Denali National Park

Glaucus gentian, Denali N.P.

Spirits Among the Blooms

Mother grizzly nurses her two cubs of the year in a field of mountain avens, Thorofare Pass, Denali N.P.

Black bear nibbles on fresh greens and new blossoms on a hillside of lupine, Chilkat Pass, Yukon.

Bumblebees, the common name given to large hairy bees, often range farther north and higher in altitude than other bees. Besides being large and hairy, queen and worker bumblebees have a special ability to shiver their flight muscles to warm themselves, better enabling them to work in cold weather than honey bees.

Bumblebees are important pollinators of flowers and food crops. Fifty species of bumblebees are known in North America. Their various sizes, colors, and body shapes are adapted to gathering nector from a diversity of specific plants. Close examination will reveal two different bumble bee species in the images on this page.

Although bumblebees collect nectar and store it as honey, they do not hoard large amounts of it as do honey bees. Their colonies have fewer bees than the colonies of honey bees and do not survive the winter. The queen hibernates alone during winter to begin a new colony in the spring.

Bumblebee hovers in flight over fireweed.

Bumblebee gathers nectar from fireweed blossom.

Individual Spirits

Red fox kit investigates its surroundings, Polychrome Pass, Denali National Park.

Year old wolf pup heads back to den near Toklat, Denali N.P., June.

Bull moose gathers energy for the mating season, Denali National Park, late August.

Dall sheep ram basks peacefully in the soft evening light, Polychrome Pass, Denali National Park.

Bull caribou wanders across autumn tundra near Fish Creek, Denali National Park.

Five month old wolf pup from the Toklat pack stops to howl, Polychrome Pass, Denali National Park.

Cross-fox pauses near Stony Hill, Denali National Park.

Porcupine steps out of the dark brush for a brief moment to investigate the call of a human voice, interior Alaska.

Young bull moose feeds on fresh greens, between Tok and Delta Junction, Alaska.

Family Spirits

Grizzly and cubs of the year (COY's), Denali N.P., August

Grizzly and COY, Denali National Park, June

Moose cow and calf, Denali National Park, June

Mountain goat and kid, Jasper N.P., June

Caribou and calf, Thorofare Pass, Denali National Park, September

Great-horned owlet stretches its wings, Sanctuary River, Denali National Park, June.

Willow ptarmigan and chicks, Denali National Park, June

Swan and cygnet, Haines, AK. June

Three young mallards, Pickhandle Lake, Yukon, August

Double Page Spread Next Two Pages:
Swans rest in the Upper Copper River Delta in the Chugach Mountains above Cordova, Alaska, May.

Winged Spirits

Raven in flight, Polychrome Pass, Denali National Park

Northern hawk owl, Denali National Park

Great blue heron stands watch on rock in Chilkoot Lake, Haines, AK.

Right top to bottom: Harlequin duck, Portage Cove, Haines, Alaska; Pacific loon, Scottie Creek, Yukon; Pair ring-necked ducks, Mirror Creek, Yukon; Pair common loons, Denali N.P.; Black-bellied plover, Chilkat estuary, Alaska

Sandhill cranes begin their migration south, Alaska, September.

Trumpeter swan sends another swan away from its mate, interior Alaska, May.

Snow geese and greater white-fronted geese mingle at Chilkat estuary, Alaska, May.

Spirits of the Council Grounds

Bald eagles gather in cottonwoods along the Chilkat River, Chilkat Bald Eagle Preserve, Alaska.

Juvenile bald eagle, Chilkat River

Bald eagles, Chilkat River Council Grounds, and Klukwan village

Bald eagle, Chilkat Bald Eagle Preserve, Alaska

Three great rivers, the Chilkat, Tsirku, and Klehini come together 21 miles north of Haines, Alaska, along the Haines Highway, at a place commonly referred to as the "Council Grounds" in the Chilkat Bald Eagle Preserve just downriver from the Tlingit village of Klukwan. Here upwellings of spring water from deep glacially-formed gravel beds create an ice-free area into which chum salmon return as late as January when other parts of these three rivers and rivers elsewhere are frozen over. Thousands of eagles from Alaska and beyond are attracted to the area for the accessible late-season salmon feast. Eagle numbers peak here in November when the surrounding waters begin to freeze.

Bald eagle feeds on salmon from the Chilkat River, Alaska.

A Diversity of Traits and Talents

Tree squirrel, Gerstle River, Alaska

Grizzly and cubs nap in meadow, Thorofare Pass, Denali N.P.

Grizzly digs roots of wild pea, Denali N.P.

Young elk, southwest of Whitehorse, Yukon

Coyote, south of Beaver Creek, Yukon

Caribou with blood red antlers from freshly shed velvet, AK

Dall sheep ram, Denali N.P.

Hoary marmot, Denali N.P.

Red fox, Denali National Park

Arctic ground squirrel, Denali N.P.

Cross-fox in willow blooms, Denali National Park

Black bear, north of Burwash, Yukon

Two moose in winter, Chilkat Pass, British Columbia

Spirits of Migration Corridors

Dall sheep pause near Fish Creek as they cross the tundra of Thorofare Pass in Denali National Park in September. Thorofare Pass is one of the significant migration corridors of the Park for herd animals such as Dall sheep and caribou, many of whom spend their summers on the north slopes of the Alaska Range and their winters on the south facing slopes of neighboring mountains of somewhat lower elevation. The many migration corridors of the North are important to the health and diversity of individuals, species, and herds.

Caribou move across a ridge of Thorofare Pass, Denali National Park, September.

Small Spirits

Robin on budding poplar, Haines, Alaska

Gray jay on spruce top, Denali National Park

Stellar's jay, winter, Chilkat River, Alaska

Young Bonaparte gull, Chilkoot Lake, late summer

Adult Bonaparte gull, Chilkoot estuary, spring

The Chilkoot River attracts multitudes of migrating and resident gulls in spring, especially during the hooligan (eulachon) run. In late summer and autumn, the Chilkoot River system again becomes an important feeding area for migrating gulls, this time returning with their young and utilizing late season runs of salmon.

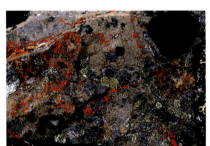
Varied colored lichens on rock, Denali National Park

Swallowtail butterfly on Lapland rosebay, Denali N.P.

Dragonfly, Yarger Lake, Tetlin Wildlife Refuge

Spotted sandpipers, Alaska: Adult, Haines (left), Chick, Yarger Lake (center), Egg, Haines (right)

Youthful Spirits

SAGA work crew, assigned to build a trail in Gustavus, takes some advance time to explore Yarger Lake and points beyond in Alaska.

Kiteboarder catches some frigid early season wind, Kluane Lake, Yukon.

Young man in Fairbanks, Alaska, gives first-class treatment to dogs he adopted after finding them abandoned along a roadside.

Young boy, taking in the scenery, becomes part of it, Kluane Lake, Yukon.

Spirits of Tradition

David Andrews at eagle release, Haines, Alaska

Art Johns, Tagish, Yukon, in Juneau, Alaska

Marilyn Wilson, Margaret Stevens, Josie Johnson--friends at the SE Alaska State Fair

Alaska residents gather along the Twenty Mile River, south of Anchorage, to dipnet nutrient-rich hooligan (eulachon), May.

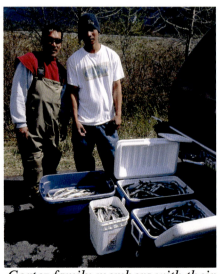

Cortez family members with their hooligan from Twenty Mile River

Totem, Chief Shakes Island, Wrangell, Alaska

Orca petroglyph, Wrangell, Alaska

Friendship totem, Whitehorse, Yukon

Traces of Spirits

Cottonwood leaf on sand flats formations of Klehini River, near Porcupine, Alaska

Ptarmigan wings on tundra, Denali N.P.

Chum salmon carcass, Chilkat River, Alaska

Lynx tracks at Lynx Creek, between Fort McPherson and Inuvik, Northwest Territories

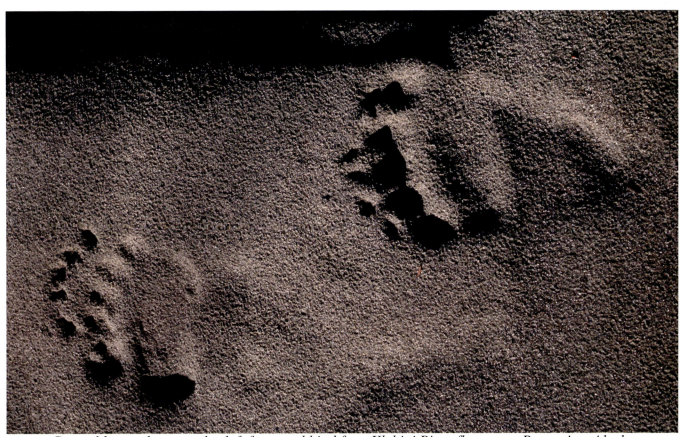
Coastal brown bear tracks, left front and hind feet, Klehini River flats, near Porcupine, Alaska

Spirits of Color

Colors are nature's way of taking advantage of selected parts of the light spectrum. Some colors of light are absorbed and some colors are reflected to our eyes.

Spring and summer's greens, through chlorophyll, reflect green light back to our eyes as plants absorb the red, yellow, and orange wavelengths of light to transform light energy into food during the growing season. The underlying reds, oranges, and yellows are revealed in autumn as green fades away. Leaves detach and fall so that plants can conserve energy during the frozen, dormant season of winter.

On a clear day, the sky appears blue because the atmosphere surrounding the earth scatters the shorter blue light wavelengths more than they scatter the longer red and yellow light wavelengths. Where the atmosphere becomes more dense, such as through our line of vision at sunset, more of the longer wavelength reds, oranges, and yellows are reflected to our eyes.

Rainbows, through prisms of water droplets, split the sun's pure white light into its components.

Flowering plants have evolved with varying colors in their blooms as specific adaptations for attracting specific pollinators.

Nature's colors are displayed in the landscape and sky of Denali National Park, September.

Tundra in autumn reveals the hidden colors in its diverse foliage, near the Arctic Circle, Yukon.

Double rainbow, Kootenay National Park, British Columbia

The greens of spring show vividly at Kluane World Heritage Site near Klukshu, Yukon.

Two moose wander through the autumn foliage, Denali National Park, Alaska.

Spirits of North Winds

Sleet blows onto partially frozen Chilkoot Lake, Alaska, January.

Patterns in the snow, Chilkat Pass, British Columbia, March

Fireweed seeds being scattered by the wind, Denali N.P., late August

Frosted wild celery, Chilkat River, Alaska

Fireweed leaves, Yarger Lake, Tetlin Wildlife Refuge, Alaska, September

Ice crystals at spring break-up, Kluane Lake, Yukon, May

Wind blows across the tundra and taiga of Chilkat Pass, British Columbia, September.

Spirits of Music and Dance

Luke Laferte from Whitehorse, Yukon, adds some French Canadian spirit to Alaska Folk Festival in Juneau, Alaska.

Jim Stey and Peter Zug play old-time fiddle in Juneau, Alaska.

The Pimentos of Haines, Alaska, entertain at the Tribal House.

Jerry Alfred from the Yukon brings his music to a special Native American Art and Music Festival in Haines, Alaska.

The Preserves, a Juneau group, perform at Alaska Folk Festival.

Klukwan Chilkats celebrate their tradition at the Alaska Native Sisterhood Hall in Klukwan, Alaska.

Young Chilkat Dancers perform on stage, Chilkat Center, Haines, Alaska.

Connecting Spirits

Adult lynx at Kroshel's park

Steve Kroschel talks wolverine talk.

Kroshel's three month old lynx kits

Animals elusive in the wild, such as lynx, wolverine, marten, mink, lemming, and some large raptors, adapt to human interaction and provide deeper insight into their personalities under the care and training of Steve Kroschel and Mario Benassi at Kroschel's wildlife park near Haines, Alaska. The young wolverine shown here is one of twin males born at Kroschel's park. Kroschel has raised wolverines for over thirty years and during this time has successfully bred and reared four litters of wolverines in captivity, a rare accomplishment.

Mario Benassi with red-tailed hawk

Kroschel demonstrates the affectionate side of a wolverine.

Working Creatively

Dan Humphrey, Haines, draws pure birch syrup.

Mel Harvey, Nenana, tends a hive of honeybees.

Ray Menaker, Haines, spins a variety of yarns, confident that his wife, Vivian, will soon knit something soft for him to wear.

Buster Benson at his sawmill, rain or shine, Haines, Alaska

Spirits of Flowing Waters

Cascading falls, north of Highway Pass, Denali National Park

Million Dollar Falls, Takahanne River, 99-Mile Haines Highway, Yukon

Bald eagle and chum salmon, Klehini River, Haines, Alaska.

Sockeye salmon leaps up Moricetown Falls in British Columbia as local villager readies his net.

Sockeye salmon in spawning colors, Bear Creek, Upper Chilkoot Watershed, Haines, Alaska

Spirits of Transition

Snowshoe hare exchanges winter's white for summer's brown, Denali N.P., June.

Transitioning snowshoe hare blends perfectly with spring grasses, Denali N.P., June.

Snowshoe hare's winter ears contrast with the red leaves of autumn in a year lacking a typical early snowfall, Teklanika Campground, Denali National Park, September.

Male rock ptarmigan, spring

Young willow ptarmigan, autumn

Willow ptarmigan chick, June

Alaska's three species of ptarmigan--willow, rock, and white-tailed--molt seasonally to blend into the landscape. All turn white in winter, with the rock ptarmigan generally having a distinctive black band across its eye. White-tailed ptarmigan, the most rare, are adapted to higher altitudes. Their summer colors blend with the talus of the high country. Male ptarmigan, with their brighter colors, distract predators from their mates and chicks. The females' colors are more muted for better hiding.

Male willow ptarmigan, among dwarf willows, Denali N.P., June

Female white-tailed ptarmigan, Denali N.P., June

Male white-tailed ptarmigan, Denali N.P., June

Two Spirits, Four Seasons

Grizzly and her yearling, June 2006

Same pair with cub as two-year old, June 2007

Close-up of two-year old Paprika, June 2007

The two bears featured here first caught my eye in mid-June of 2006. I spotted them again at least once in each of the subsequent seasons of 2007, 2008, and 2009. They were distinctive, seeming to prefer grazing on the green grasses of Sable Valley while most other grizzly bears I had observed in Denali National Park at this time of year seemed to prefer digging up the roots of the wild pea in Thorofare Pass or Savage River flats. Over the seasons, I became familiar with their coloring, their body type, and their mannerisms. Due to their coloring, I named the mother Coffee and the cub Paprika. By 2008, the cub was on its own. I observed both mother and cub grazing in Sable Valley in 2008 and 2009, though only alone and on different days from each other.

Grizzly bears generally inhabit specific territories. Their preferred regions may change over the seasons and years, depending on other bears in the vicinity and availability of food. Typically, a young grizzly will be forced away from its mother at the age of three. The mother may mate again the following spring. If conditions are right, she will likely give birth the spring after that. Grizzly cubs take six to seven years to fully mature.

Coffee scratches her back on willows in Sable Valley in autumn of 2008.

Three year old Paprika, June 2008

Four year old Paprika, June 2009

Coffee munches on tundra blueberries, Sable Valley, autumn 2008.

Spirits of Sable Valley

Late summer, Sable Valley, Denali National Park and conditions including stormy skies and fireweed in full bloom create a moment in time and place unlike any other.

Though ever-changing, Sable Valley, set aside as critical wildlife habitat, provides consistent and secure habitat for an abundance of wild plants, animals, and birds.

Wolves, wolverine, fox, grizzlies, caribou, moose, Dall sheep, snowshoe hares, and Arctic ground squirrels are some of the four-legged spirits that make their home in this place.

Song birds and willow ptarmigan abound. Golden eagles build nests and rear their young here.

Plants of the tundra, taiga, and high alpine area thrive in the diversity of ecological niches that thrive in this protected, wild area.

The ever-evolving dramatic circle of life, birth, death, and the struggle for survival become one eternal moment in this place.

Sable Valley with fireweed in the foreground, Denali National Park, late August

Spirits of the High Country

Mount Sanford, an ice-capped volcano in Wrangell-Saint Elias Park and Preserve, rises high above the Copper River headwaters in southcentral Alaska.

Mount Drum, the massive peak farthest west in Wrangell-Saint Elias Park and Preserve, exhibits a soft glow at sunset, southcentral Alaska.

The Matanuska Glacier flows out of the Chugach Mountains into the Matanuska River of southcentral Alaska.

Tracks of skiers highlight this snowfield on Thompson Pass in the Chugach Mountains north of Valdez, Alaska.

Arctic ground squirrel (left) takes in the view from Highway Pass, Denali National Park. Denali with a fresh mantle of snow (above) towers behind Stony Dome, Highway Pass, Denali National Park.

Pikas

Pika gathers vegetation for the winter.

Pikas, related to rabbits and hares, live in high altitude talus rock slopes. They gather vegetation, stack it outside in piles to dry, and store it in burrows for winter. These collared pikas, the northernmost American pika species, make their home near Eielson in Denali National Park.

Pika checks out its surroundings.

Pika calls out its distinctive whistle.

Pika nibbles on coltsfoot.

Glacial Spirits

Ice breaks away from actively calving South Sawyer Glacier, Tracy Arm, Inside Passage, Alaska.

Collapse of face of South Sawyer Glacier, Tracy Arm, leaves huge hole and creates new icebergs.

Harbor seals haul out on icebergs near South Sawyer Glacier.

Icebergs stranded in the shallows of Alaska's Inside Passage near the entrance to Tracy Arm exhibit colors and forms influenced by the weather and tides.

Mountain Spirits

Clouds nestle in the Cathedral Peaks of the Chilkat Range, Haines, Alaska.

Denali, the highest peak in North America, rises above the Alaska Range, Denali National Park.

Ocean and Pond Spirits

Tall dorsal fins mark a pod of transient orcas investigating the waters of Chilkat Inlet, Haines, Alaska.

Sea otter cradles clam on belly, Cordova, Alaska.

Harbor seal with salmon, Haines, Alaska

Sea lion family, Haines, Alaska

Beaver hauls twigs to its home in a high alpine pond, Denali N.P.

Pigeon guillemot, Valdez, Alaska.

Spirits Bid Adieu

Mother humpack whale rolls across the surface as her calf shows its tail before diving deep into the ocean waters of Alaska's Inside Passage.

Books by Kathleen M.K. Menke/Crystal Images Photography and Publishing

PO Box 781, Haines, Alaska 99827   ci@akmk.com   www.akmk.com

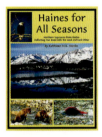

Haines for All Seasons--Northern Exposures from
Alaska Reflecting Our Bond to the Land and Each Other
200 original color images in and around Haines, Alaska, 1985-2005
Scenics, wildlife, cultural tradition, community, and more
   "A magnificent publication!"
      Genevieve Hetu, Heritage Communicator, Kluane World Heritage Site, Yukon
Additional reviews and online ordering information: **www.akmk.com/hfas**

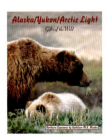

Alaska/Yukon/Arctic Light-- Book of Year Award
Gifts of the Wild   Finalist 2007--"Nature"
175 original color images celebrating life, light, and landscape in the Far North as
the seasons progress from spring break-up full circle to early spring once again.
   **"I just had to say thanks! I've spent a fair amount of my spare time in
   the last 50 years "capturing the light" ... and your new book does
   just that ... at a place near and dear to my heart and spirit."**
      Richard Voss, Refuge Manager, Arctic National Wildlife Refuge, Alaska
Additional reviews and online ordering information: **www.akmk.com/ayal**

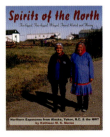

Spirits of the North--Two-legged, Four-legged,
Winged, Finned, Rooted, and Flowing
   "Outstanding book. An insightful portrayal of 'spirit.'"
      Alan Traut, Docent, Sheldon Museum and Cultural Center, Haines, Alaska
Additional reviews and online ordering information: **www.akmk.com/son**